GRILLAHOLICS
STUFFED
BURGER PRESS

Recipes of the **50** UNITED STATES

DELICIOUS Cookbook
FOR YOUR GRILLING
BBQ HAMBURGER
PATTY MAKER from
Every State In
the USA

Richard Erwin & Tasha Spencer

LEGAL NOTICE

This information contained in this book is for entertainment purposes only. The content represents the opinion of the author and is based on the author's personal experience and observations. The author does not assume any liability whatsoever for the use of or inability to use any or all information contained in this book, and accepts no responsibility for any loss or damages of any kind that may be incurred by the reader as a result of actions arising from the use of the information in this book. Use this information at your own risk. No part of this book may be reproduced or transmitted in any form or by any means, electronic or mechanical, including photocopying, recording, or by any information storage or retrieval system, without express written permission from the author, except in the case of brief quotations embodied in critical articles and reviews – or except by a reviewer who may quote brief passages in a review.

The author reserves the right to make any changes he or she deems necessary to future versions of the publication to ensure its accuracy.

Published In The United States of America By Healthy Lifestyle Recipes
www.Healthylifestylerecipes.org

BEFORE TURNING THE PAGE

FREE Cookbooks

If you like new cookbooks then we want to wet your whistle with **"FREE"** recipes from books that we publish! **This is our appreciation** for you having an interest in this book. We want to give you the opportunity to receive others that we publish for **FREE** by joining our exclusive recipe book club: **"Cookbook Fanatics!"**

Turn to the back of the book for more details!

Don't want to wait...just click the link below to get started...Enjoy!

"Additional Marinades"

Yours FREE for signing up to Our List!

Get My Free Book

www.Healthylifestylerecipes.org/Freebook2review

INTRODUCTION

This book will have you cooking like a pro in no time! These recipes are designed to take your level of cooking to another level, by "Keepin it Crispy!". You will notice when using this safe non stick cookware is the only way you should be making meals your kitchen! This book will quickly give you the expertise you need to fully enjoy the benefits of non stick cuisine. Today's reader wants quick, short and easy to read paragraphs to make cooking simple but fun, and that's what we have done with this recipe book.

We also have a little bonus section for those who like marinades for that mouth watering smack in the mouth flavor that you only thought you could get at those 5 star restaurants. But now it's possible in the comfort of your own kitchen! Extraordinary flavor foods with the taste of bliss, and it's all you'll every need right here at your fingertips!

Show everyone that you are the master in your kitchen. They will think you spent hours to whip up some of these delicious tidbits.

Now...Get Cooking, and **May the Crisp Be with You!**

TABLE OF CONTENTS

BURGERS FROM EVERY STATE IN THE UNITED STATES

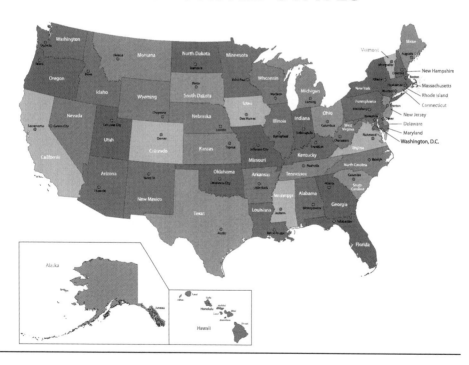

BPA Free Material – Smart, Safe And Sensible!

One of the main concerns of plastic kitchenware is whether or not the accessory contains Bisphenol A, a common chemical used to harden plastics. We are still unaware of definite effects caused by the chemical, but we have come to the point where it does pose risks to one's health. It can affect the brain, gland, and behavior if someone is overexposed. With that being said, the Grillaholics Stuffed Burger Press is proud to say that the product is BPA free!

It's easy to use, safe, and very easy to clean. You can hand wash the press of simply put it in the dishwasher because it is also dishwasher safe to add to its list of great benefits. This is perfect for entertaining so you don't have to spend time in the kitchen after dinner which means more time spent with friends and family.

A Perfect Pressed Circle...Every Time!

A burger is pretty basic to make and is noticeable to everyone. No one has ever asked, "Hey, what's this round thing on the plate?" However, how often do you see a perfectly round burger outside of a freezer at the grocery store? Rarely.

The Grillaholics Stuffed Burger press has a solid round design that allows you to create a perfect sealed circle of a STUFFED, BEEFED UP patty. One of the rare complaints people have ordering a hamburger while dining out is that the bun does not match the size or shape of the patty. This is different than the hot dog and hot dog pun packaging ratio conundrum; this is something that can be fixed with the right tool. You have that tool now!

HOW TO USE YOU'RE BURGER PRESS

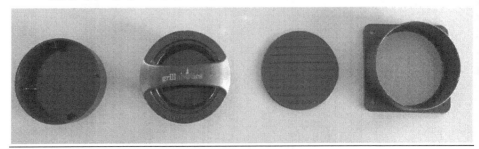

Easy As 1-2-3

Being a master burger stuffer doesn't have to be hard; it's actually quite simple. You can make delicious burgers in a matter of three easy steps! We already covered the simple design of the Grillaholics Stuffed Burger Press, now let's talk quickly about how to use it. You have your ingredients ready so it's time to make some burgers!

1) Prepare your meat by dividing into sections and rounding into balls. Try not to exceed a ½ pound. Then divide each ball into a large piece and a slightly smaller one; about 60%/40% give or take.

2) Place the larger piece of meat in the Grillaholics Stuffed Burger Press. Next, remove the bottom cap from the top lid to access the cavity creator. Press down on the meat making a perfectly round and deep crater directly in the center, and then add the ingredients of your liking to the hole.

3) Take the smaller piece of meat and seal the top, trapping the ingredients within. Re-cap the top lid to create a flat base once again, cover and press down. Make sure to trim any excess meat that forms around the rim. Remove the lid and simply release the burger by pressing on the bottom tray. Transfer to

> Place the other patty on top of the other patty
> Use the SEAL side of the Burger Press to keep the two patties in place. Close the press firmly, which will seal the patties together. Release the press.
> Put the patties on the grill and cook for 6 minutes on each side
> Place the burger on a bun and top with a piece of catfish. Serve with toppings of your choice.

Presentation Matters

When you think of burgers you don't usually affiliate gourmet with them whether it be the taste or atmosphere. Outside with the fixings atop a table and a paper plate to hold your meal is a common setting. Now that you're experienced with your Stuffed Burger Press, you might as well go all out!

Presentation matters, well sometimes, but for this section's sake it does. Let's say you made a turkey burger stuffed with feta, onions, and spinach. You placed a sliced tomato and an avocado wedge on top and stick everything between a divided buttered brioche. This deserves a classy display! Position nicely on a plate and garnish with fresh parsley or oregano. Even better yet...get a stick of rosemary and push it down the middle of the burger to hold together the masterpiece you've just created! People will rave about their dining experience, and you can stick around for the "Standing Ovation!" but don't forget to leave room for sides and to pair with your favorite drink!

Of course, as stated, presentation only sometimes matter. If you're making delicious stuffed burgers then the setting really doesn't matter.

THE "STUFF" OF PRO'S

Marinade That Meat

One of the wonderful aspects of meat is that it's very versatile. So many flavors can combine to give you a delightful taste, and even ingredients like onions and garlic are also adaptable enough to go with any meat or vegetable. It's a win-win! However, the key to juicy flavorful patties is marinating.

Marinating is a technique that comes highly-recommended. The pros do it all the time and the reason being is so the meat soaks up all the flavor, but one important aspect to marinating is time. The longer the burger soaks, the more flavor it absorbs. Sometimes I even marinate 24-hours in advance!

With the Grillaholics Stuffed Burger Press it's easy. First make your delicious patty, marinade in your choice of sauce*, and then wrap to store or place on the grill or pan. Either way, the flavor will give your burgers an extra pop! Worcestershire sauce, honey, teriyaki, barbeque, the possibilities are endless!

*you may also marinade the meat before using the burger press.

In addition to ingredients and preparation, you must also be precise with your cooking. Different meats require different times on the grill or pan, and eaters have different tastes and styles they prefer. Here is a small table for reference:

DONENESS	BEEF & LAMB	POULTRY	PORK
Rare (Cool Red Center)	125 Degrees	n/a	n/a
Medium Rare (Warm Red Center)	130-135 Degrees	n/a	145 Degrees
Medium (Warm Pink Center)	135-140 Degrees	n/a	150 Degrees
Medium Well (Slightly Pink Center)	140-150 Degrees	n/a	155 Degrees
Well Done (Little or no Pink)	155+ Degrees	165-175 Degrees	160 Degrees

Don't undercook, don't overcook, don't make them too moist, and don't make them too dry. It takes precision to be a pro.

PUTTING UP THE LEFTOVERS

Wrap It Up

Food storage is actually a science. Well, maybe not actually, you can't major in it or anything, but the proper way to seal your leftovers and organize your refrigerator is important knowledge to have. Since you will be using your Grillaholics Stuffed Burger Press often there will be leftovers.

First, leftovers should be sealed and stored no more than two hours after you have finished cooking. Also, modern refrigerators prevent you from having to wait until your food cools; you can store it right away if you want!

It's vital that you use leak-proof containers and storage bags or quality plastic wrap, assuring that all your leftovers are airtight. If you use smaller separate containers to divide your leftovers then it will not take as long to cool which prevents contamination from certain bacteria even more, and try to remove as much air as possible before sealing.

Channel Your Inner Tetris

A clean and organized refrigerator is a happy one; it also means a happy wife from personal experience, but that is beside the point. Arranging your food products and leftovers properly is an art, but also very important. Vegetables, dairy, meat, eggs, everything has its own area!

Let's start with the shelving. You didn't know it mattered? Well, it does and there is a method behind the madness. You should store most leftovers on the upper shelves as well as drinks, dairy products, and foods that are essentially ready to consume and don't need to be cooked like vegetables and breads. The bottom shelves should be reserved for raw meats and other ingredients used for cooking that may be prone to drip. If you can't fit all your raw ingredients on the very bottom shelf, simply place a plate underneath the food just in case!

Now to the drawers and door. That's right, it's not over yet! The door should solely be used for condiments because it's actually the warmest part of the fridge so it would be wise not to place anything that requires cold temperatures or is perishable on the small shaves; things like milk and eggs for example. Drawers are also quite specific because they are meant to hold certain products depending on their respective humidity needed to stay fresh. Example: fruits and vegetables. Still be careful of meats resting above though if the drawers are on the bottom; there is still a risk of contamination. That's where the aforementioned plate comes in handy again!

Your refrigerator should remain below 40 degrees, try not to overload the fridge because it obstructs circulation of the cold air, and make sure you eat your meat leftovers within four days. You don't want your "New Burger Creations" to go to waste! Writing the date down and keeping them towards the front of the refrigerator is a handy reminder.

Destroy The Evidence

Don't worry, a crime hasn't been committed, unless of course someone stole your burger recipes and secrets which would be awful. You know you can clean your Grillaholics Stuffed Burger Press easily, but what about the rest?

There won't be much mess because the simplicity of the press, but there will be some spillage during preparation, and it is very important to clean up after the fact. You don't have to stop you're cooking to tend to the counter, but you can tidy up during and really clean after.

The extra minutes you have while your burgers are cooking can be used to wash some of your prep dishes and pick up and dispose of any stray ingredients. It will keep the kitchen tidy, and save you time after you've enjoyed your delicious meal.

Handling and cooking with raw meat has potential health risks that is why making sure the dish is cooked enough is vital, but also cleaning the juices that leaked during preparation is just as important. Use a disinfecting wipe or spray to assure that your counter is clear of bacteria such as E. coli, salmonella, and listeria. You don't want that stuff ruining a good thing. Gross!

Enjoy!

There's really only one last thing to do: Enjoy your creations! You may have gone a little overboard with your Grillaholics Stuffed Burger Press the night before, but that's not your fault; it's easy and fun to use so you're allowed to get carried away. However, if you didn't stuff yourself silly then you get to enjoy the meals the next day.

Whether you scramble the burger into your eggs in the morning, bring it to work for lunch to make everyone in the office jealous, or just relive your dinner memories from the night before it will be easy to remind yourself how good your burger is. You're a master so be proud of it!

AMAZING UNIQUE RECIPES!

When reading these recipes just remember that you are reading the views and opinions of the writer. We have also provided pretty creative Stuffed Burger Recipes for you Burger Lovers out there." So, Turn the page, "Dive - Head First" and get Grilling! :)

Alaska: Buttery Mouthwatering Salmon Burger

There's just something about freshly-caught salmon from the Northwest. Cold waters and huge fish equal a flaky and tender main course. You don't have to swim way up-stream to get it either. Enjoy the Last Frontier in your backyard.

Prep Time: 15 Minutes
Cook Time: 40 Minutes
Servings: 6

INGREDIENTS:

Sweet potato fries:
3 large sweet potatoes
2 tablespoon canola oil
1 ½ teaspoon salt
2 tbsp. Cajun seasoning

Burger:
1 (16 ounce) can salmon, drained and flaked
2 eggs
¼ cup chopped fresh parsley
2 tablespoons finely chopped onion
¼ cup Italian seasoned dry bread crumbs
2 tablespoons lemon juice
1/3 teaspoon dried basil
1 pinch red pepper flakes
1 tablespoon vegetable oil

Dressing:
2 tablespoons light mayonnaise
1 tablespoon lemon juice
1tablespoon melted butter
1 pinch dried basil

DIRECTIONS:

> Sweet Potato Fries: Set the oven to 450 degrees
> Peel the potatoes and chop of the ends.
> Cut them in half lengthwise and then cut into ½ wedges.
> Combine the potatoes in a bowl and mix with the oil, salt and spices.
> Then spread on a baking sheet and bake for 25 minutes.
> Set aside.
> Combine all burger ingredients into a bowl.
> Form the mixture into six 4 ounce balls. Create each ball into a patty by using the STUFF side of the burger press to push it down.
> Put the patties on the grill and cook for 6 minutes on each side
> Combine all of the dressing ingredients into a small bowl.
> Serve on a bun with and spread the dressing on top for flavor.
> Pair with the sweet potatoes to add a little sweetness to the meal.

Arizona: Crazy for Sizzling Hot Chimichangas Burger

I think we all agree that burritos are great, right? How about deep-frying a burrito then? Of course it's good, and that's why you can't go wrong with a chimichanga. The Southwest is known for its spicy Mexican cuisine, so it's only appropriate to put it between a bun and combine cultures.

Prep Time: 5 Minutes
Cook Time: 20 Minutes
Servings: 4

INGREDIENTS:

Chimichanga Mix:
1 pound ground chicken
½ cup refried beans
½ cup chopped onion
½ cup chopped tomatoes
½ chopped bell peppers
½ teaspoon chopped garlic
Salt to taste
Pepper to taste

Burger:
½ pound ground cubed steak
Kosher Salt
Fresh Ground Pepper
1 Package Taco seasoning
2 full green onions, diced
1 full tomato, diced
1 full onion, diced
½ cup of cilantro, chopped
Sour cream
4 Kaiser Rolls, halved

DIRECTIONS:

> Combine the chimichanga mixture together in a bowl and set aside.
> Mix the ground cubed steak with the salt, pepper and taco seasoning
> Form the ground cubed steak mixture into eight 4 ounce balls. Create each ball into a patty by using the STUFF side of the burger press to push it down.
> Fill 1 of the patties with ¼ of the chimichanga mixture.
> Place the other patty on top of the other patty
> Use the SEAL side of the Burger Press to keep the two patties in place. Close the press firmly, which will seal the patties together. Release the press.
> Put the patties on the grill and cook for 6 minutes on each side.
> Serve in a bun and top with sour cream, tomato, onion and cilantro.

Arkansas: Tender Chopped Razorback Mixed Beef Burger

In the United States, beef reigns and there is absolutely nothing wrong with that. It even rules razorback country. Arkansas is a hidden American gem, and their culinary creations with our most prized cuisine will always leave you wanting more from the state.

Prep Time: 5 Minutes
Cook Time: 20 Minutes
Servings: 4

INGREDIENTS:

1 pound ground beef
1 pound ground wild boar (razorback)
Kosher Salt
Fresh Ground Pepper
½ cup French fries
1 tsp. garlic pepper
8 servings of sourdough buns, split and toasted

DIRECTIONS:

> Mix the ground beef and boar with salt and pepper separately
> Form the ground beef mixture and ground boar into four 4 ounce balls. Create each ball into a patty by using the STUFF side of the burger press to push it down.
> Top 1 of the beef patties with a quarter of the French fries.
> Place one ground bacon patty on top of the ground beef patty
> Use the SEAL side of the Burger Press to keep the two patties in place. Close the press firmly, which will seal the patties together. Release the press.
> Put the patties on the grill and cook for 6 minutes on each side.
> Serve on the sourdough and top with ketchup, yellow mustard and onion slices.

California: Awesome Fresh and Zingy Avocado Turkey Burger

I know what you're thinking, California has everything. It's true, and somewhat unfair, but luckily for the rest of the country, their fruits are fresh, and nothing beats a ripe Californian avocado. Slice it up and rest atop a patty, and your burger goes from good to amazing.

Prep Time: 5 Minutes
Cook Time: 20 Minutes
Servings: 6

INGREDIENTS:
Avocado Spread:
Pinch of minced garlic
1 teaspoon of lemon juice
1 teaspoon chopped tomatoes
1 teaspoon Kalamata olives
1 ½ ripe avocado, sliced

Burger:
2 lbs. lean ground turkey
3 green onions, finely chopped
2 cloves garlic, minced
2 tablespoons fresh parsley, finely chopped
1 tablespoon fresh sage, finely chopped
2 tablespoons Dijon mustard
2 large eggs
¼ cup almond flour
1 teaspoon salt
½ teaspoon ground white pepper

DIRECTIONS:

> Burgers: Combine all burger ingredients into a bowl.
> Cut the avocados in half and slice into three slices. Toss the remaining parts of the avocado into another bowl.
> Combine all of the avocado mixture together and smash with a fork.
> Form the mixture into twelve 4 ounce balls. Create each ball into a patty by using the STUFF side of the burger press to push it down.
> Fill 1 of the patties with ¼ of the avocado mixture in the center of the patty.
> Place the other patty on top of the other patty
> Use the SEAL side of the Burger Press to keep the two patties in place. Close the press firmly, which will seal the patties together. Release the press.
> Put the patties on the grill and cook for 6 minutes on each side.
> Serve on a bun and top with lettuce, caramelized onions and sautéed mushrooms.

Colorado: Mile High Fiery Mouthful Burgers

Coloradans are generally healthy, but still indulge. For example, they don't deep-fry their burritos, but rather leave them be. Fair enough. Breakfast and Chile Verde burritos reign supreme in the Rocky Mountains, so why not combine both and put it in between a bun for good measure?

Prep Time: 5 Minutes
Cook Time: 20 Minutes
Servings: 4

INGREDIENTS:
Chili Verde:
1 ½ lbs. pork chorizo
1 can chopped green chilies
2 tablespoons onion, chopped
2 tablespoons tomato, chopped
1 bundle of cilantro, chopped
1 tablespoon flour
¼ teaspoon cumin
¼ teaspoon oregano
¼ teaspoon garlic salt
1 cube chicken bouillon
1/3 cup water

1½ lbs. ground beef
Kosher Salt
Fresh Ground Pepper
½ shredded cheddar cheese
4 English Muffins, toasted and split
Salsa, for tasting

DIRECTIONS:

> Combine the chili Verde ingredients together in a bowl. Set aside
> Mix the ground beef with salt and pepper
> Form the ground bacon mixture into eight 4 ounce balls. Create each ball into a patty by using the STUFF side of the burger press to push it down.
> Fill 1 of the patties with a quarter of the chili Verde mix.
> Place the other patty on top of the other patty
> Use the SEAL side of the Burger Press to keep the two patties in place. Close the press firmly, which will seal the patties together. Release the press.
> Put the patties on the grill and cook for 6 minutes on each side.
> Serve on the English Muffins and top with salsa.

Connecticut: Creamy Cheese and Clam Pizza Pie Pork Burger

People tend to forget that Connecticut has a great New York influence from food to theater. They back it up too, rivaling the Big Apple's pizza, but making it their own. It's tough to make pizza better than it already is, but Connecticut clams do the trick!

Prep Time: 5 Minutes
Cook Time: 20 Minutes
Servings: 4

INGREDIENTS:

1½ lbs. lean ground pork
Kosher Salt
Fresh Ground Pepper
½ cup garlic Alfredo sauce
1 teaspoon garlic powder
½ teaspoon dried basil or oregano, crushed
4 slices Mozzarella
1 cup real Italian Pecorino Romano Cheese
1 cup shucked clams, diced
4 Sourdough rolls, halved

DIRECTIONS:

> Combine all ingredients, but the cheese and clams.
> Form the ground pork into eight 4 ounce balls. Create each ball into a patty by using the STUFF side of the burger press to push it down.
> Fill 1 of the patties with ¼ of the clams, ¼ of the Romano cheese and 1 slice of mozzarella cheese
> Place the other patty on top of the other patty
> Use the SEAL side of the Burger Press to keep the two patties in place. Close the press firmly, which will seal the patties together. Release the press.
> Put the patties on the grill and cook for 6 minutes on each side
> Put the remaining Alfredo sauce on a top of the bun and sprinkle with Parmesan cheese.

Delaware: Succulent Stuffed Scrapple Burger

So what the heck is Scrapple? It's not a misspelled board game, that's for sure. Let's just say that Delaware doesn't waste any part of the pig. Pork, home fries, egg, and maybe some spicy ketchup makes a perfect brunch burger. The First State has been around a while; they know what they're doing.

Prep Time: 20 Minutes
Cook Time: 15 Minutes
Servings: 2

INGREDIENTS
Scrapple:
1/1/2 lbs. ground pork sausage
1 14 ounce can sweetened condensed milk
1 cup yellow cornmeal
1/8 teaspoon coarsely ground black pepper

Burger:
1 pound ground beef
4 slices American cheese
Garlic cloves, chopped 2-4
Salt to taste
Pepper to taste
2 buns, halved and grilled

DIRECTIONS:
> Scrapple: place the ground pork in a skillet.
> Cook on medium until brown.
> Drain and rinse in colander under cold water.
> Break the pork into small piece and then return to the skillet.
> Add the milk and heat over medium until it bubbles.
> Stir in the cornmeal and pepper immediately reducing the heat .
> Simmer for 5 minutes.
> Pack in a loaf pan, cover and chill overnight.
> Slice the pieces into ¼ slices.

> Burger: Form the ground beef into two 4 ounce balls. Create each ball into a patty by using the STUFF side of the burger press to push it down.
> Fill 1 of the patties with a piece of the scrapple.
> Place the other patty on top of the other patty
> Use the SEAL side of the Burger Press to keep the two patties in place. Close the press firmly, which will seal the patties together. Release the press.
> Put the patties on the grill and cook for 6 minutes on each side
> Toast your buns and add burgers to bottom buns.

Florida: Zesty Sliced Key Lime Beach Burger

You think oranges when you think Florida, I mean, the fruit is on their license plate. However, their key limes are just as juicy and popular. Lime adds a great flavor and zest to meat; it will make you feel like you're having a fresh burger on the beach, enjoying the sun and shore. A nice escape in your own backyard!

Prep Time: 5 Minutes
Cook Time: 20 Minutes
Servings: 4

INGREDIENTS:

1 ½ ground pork
4 limes, peeled and sliced
½ cup rosemary
1 carrot, shaved
1 cup of red cabbage
1 cub Napa cabbage
½ cup mayonnaise
½ cup lime juice
Salt and pepper
4 hamburger bans, split

> Directions:
> Combine the ground pork, rosemary and lime juice
> Combine the carrots, mayonnaise, and cabbage together to make a salad
> Form the ground pork into eight 4 ounce balls. Create each ball into a patty by using the STUFF side of the burger press to push it down.
> Fill 1 of the patties with one full lime.
> Place the other patty on top of the other patty
> Use the SEAL side of the Burger Press to keep the two patties in place. Close the press firmly, which will seal the patties together. Release the press.
> Put the patties on the grill and cook for 6 minutes on each side
> Place the burgers on top of a bun and top with the salad mixture.

Georgia: Juicy Georgia Peach Extravaganza Burger

Peaches are Georgia's thing, and no one has a problem with it. When the word *peach* is involved in any conversation it usually means something good – like, *life is peachy*. So why not take a chance on cooking the fruit with your meat. It may seem odd, but it will definitely sweeten up your meal and your day.

Prep Time: 5 Minutes
Cook Time: 20 Minutes
Servings: 4

INGREDIENTS:
1 ½ lbs. ground turkey
4 oranges, peeled and sliced
¼ teaspoon poultry seasoning
½ teaspoon ground pepper
½ teaspoon soy sauce
Salt to taste
4 hamburger bans, split

> Directions:
> Combine the ground turkey, poultry seasoning, black pepper, and soy sauce together.
> Form the ground pork into eight 4 ounce balls. Create each ball into a patty by using the STUFF side of the burger press to push it down.
> Fill 1 of the patties with one full orange.
> Place the other patty on top of the other patty
> Use the SEAL side of the Burger Press to keep the two patties in place. Close the press firmly, which will seal the patties together. Release the press.
> Put the patties on the grill and cook for 6 minutes on each side
> Place the burgers on top of a bun and top with mayonnaise.

Hawaii: Amazing Aloha Pineapple Stuffed Spam Burger

Spam is misunderstood like outcasts were during high school. Essentially, you need to give them (it) a chance. Hawaii is all about Spam; it's quick and can be quite juicy and tender. If you still need time developing a relationship with Spam, maybe use pineapple as a buffer. You never know what you're going to end up liking!

Prep Time: 5 Minutes
Cook Time: 20 Minutes
Servings: 4

INGREDIENTS:

1½ lbs. ground spam
Kosher Salt
Fresh Ground Pepper
½ cup of pineapple salsa
¼ Pineapple cut in quarters
8 servings of hamburger buns

DIRECTIONS:

❯ Mix the ground spam with the salt and pepper
❯ Form the ground spam mixture into eight 4 ounce balls. Create each ball into a patty by using the STUFF side of the burger press to push it down.
❯ Fill 1 of the patties with a quarter of the pineapple
❯ Place the other patty on top of the other patty
❯ Use the SEAL side of the Burger Press to keep the two patties in place. Close the press firmly, which will seal the patties together. Release the press.
❯ Put the patties on the grill and cook for 6 minutes on each side.
❯ Serve on the bun and top with some of the salsa.

Idaho: Towering Crispy Crunchy French Fry Burger

"Towering Crispy French Fry Burger"- Go ahead, tell me this doesn't sound delicious. You can't. Also, tell me you're *not* mad at yourself for *not* thinking of this sooner. You can't. Burgers and fries go together like Idaho and potatoes, so you might as well just cut out the middle man. I mean, you put ketchup on both, so even that step is saved when you combine the two.

Prep Time: 5 Minutes
Cook Time: 20 Minutes
Servings: 4

INGREDIENTS:

Bun:
1 frozen bag of straight cut French fries
Dab –N-Hold Edible Adhesive

Burger:
1 pound ground beef
1 pound ground bacon
Kosher Salt
Fresh Ground Pepper
½ cup French fries
1 tsp. garlic pepper

DIRECTIONS:

> Fry Bun: Bake the fries in the oven according to the directions. Make sure they are extra crisp.
> Glue the fries together side by side. Use 10 fries for the top and ten for the bottom.
> Use the rim of the glass to cut the fries into even circles.
> Burger: Mix the ground beef and bacon with salt and pepper separately
> Form the ground beef mixture and ground bacon into four 4 ounce balls. Create each ball into a patty by using the STUFF side of the burger press to push it down.

> Top 1 of the beef patties with a quarter of the French fries.
> Place one ground bacon patty on top of the ground beef patty
> Use the SEAL side of the Burger Press to keep the two patties in place. Close the press firmly, which will seal the patties together. Release the press.
> Put the patties on the grill and cook for 6 minutes on each side.
> Serve on the French fry bun and top with ketchup, yellow mustard and onion slices.

Illinois: Delicious Chicago Fire Deep-Dish Pizza Burger

When you think Illinois, you really think Chicago, and when you think Chicago, you think deep-dish pizza. Some may think Chicago dogs as well, but why mess with something that has already reached perfection? Because you can make a burger out of it, duh. Deep-dish pizza opens up more ingredient choices, however, so go wild, and bring your appetite.

Prep Time: 5 Minutes
Cook Time: 20 Minutes
Servings: 2

INGREDIENTS:

1½ lbs. lean ground beef
Salt to taste
Fresh Ground Pepper
½ cup Marinara Sauce
1 teaspoon garlic powder
½ teaspoon dried basil or oregano, crushed
½ lb. button mushrooms
½ teaspoon Hot Sauce
8 slices Mozzarella
8 pepperoni slices
2 ciabatta rolls, halved

DIRECTIONS:

❯ Combine the ground beef, salt, pepper, garlic powder, and oregano together.
❯ Form the ground beef eight 4 ounce balls. Create each ball into a patty by using the STUFF side of the burger press to push it down.
❯ Fill 1 of the patties with 2 pieces of pepperoni and 1 slice of mozzarella cheese
❯ Place the other patty on top of the other patty
❯ Use the SEAL side of the Burger Press to keep the two patties in place. Close the press firmly, which will seal the patties together. Release the press.

36

> Put the patties on the grill and cook for 6 minutes on each side.
> Place a piece of mozzarella on top of each patty and cook until melted.
> Put the marinara sauce on a top of the ciabatta bread.
> Top the burger with mushrooms and sprinkle with Parmesan cheese.

Indiana: Tender Pork Tenderloin Burgers

Indiana does a couple things right, one is basketball and the other is pork. Okay, there's plenty more to the state, but we're talking food here. So, turn on the game, and grill up some moist Indiana tenderloin. You won't be disappointed with this Midwestern staple.

Prep Time: 5 Minutes
Cook Time: 20 Minutes
Servings: 4

INGREDIENTS:

1 large egg white, beaten
1/3 cup panko
3 tablespoons dried cranberries, chopped
½ teaspoon poultry seasoning
1 pork tenderloin, cubed
2 tablespoons Dijon Mustard
3 tablespoons mayonnaise
1-1/2 teaspoons maple syrup
4 whole wheat buns, halved
Arugula for topping

DIRECTIONS:

> Mix the egg white, panko and poultry seasoning together.
> Pulse the pork tenderloin in a food processor until chopped.
> Add the pork to the egg mixture, along with the mustard, mayonnaise and the syrup.
> Form the ground pork into two 4 ounce balls. Create each ball into a patty by using the STUFF side of the burger press to push it down.
> Fill 1 of the patties with a quarter of the cranberries
> Place the other patty on top of the other patty
> Use the SEAL side of the Burger Press to keep the two patties in place. Close the press firmly, which will seal the patties together. Release the press.
> Put the patties on the grill and cook for 6 minutes on each side
> Serve on the bun and top with arugula, Ketchup, mustard or BBQ Sauce.

Iowa: Savory Sweet Corn Salsa Burger

"Savory Sweet Corn Burger"- Corn is as Midwestern as the corn-fed boys who come from the region. However, even big farmers enjoy the occasional vegetarian alternative. *Shhh*, don't share that information. You can make a veggie patty with sweet corn or even just top your meat; either way, it adds a great healthy taste to the dish!

Prep Time: 5 Minutes
Cook Time: 22 Minutes
Servings: 6

INGREDIENTS:

1 ½ cups walnuts, toasted
2/3 cup onion, chopped
2/3 cup fresh cilantro, snipped
2 teaspoons ground cumin
3 garlic cloves
½ teaspoon dried oregano, crushed
½ teaspoon dried basil. Crushed
2 15 ounce can black beans, rinsed and drained
¼ cup can diced green Chile peppers, drained
2 eggs, beaten
¾ cup bread crumbs
¼ teaspoon ground black pepper
6 English muffins, split

Corn Salsa:
1 can sweet corn, drained and rinsed
1 tomato, chopped
¼ cup onion, chopped
¼ cup fresh cilantro, snipped
1 teaspoon lime peel, shredded
2 tablespoons lime juice
2 tablespoons olive oil
½ fresh jalapeno Chile pepper, seeded and chopped
¼ teaspoon chopped

¼ teaspoon ground black pepper

DIRECTIONS:

> Salsa: Combine all the salsa ingredients together and set aside.
> Burger: Mix the walnuts, the onion, cilantro, cumin, garlic, oregano and basil together in a food processor.
> Add in the black beans and Chile peppers until combined.
> Place the mixture in a bowl and stir in the eggs, breadcrumbs and black pepper.
> Form the patties into six 4 ounce balls.
> Put the patties on the grill and cook for 3 minutes on each side
> Serve on a bun with ketchup, lettuce and tomato.

Kansas: Thick and Saucy Kansas BBQ Rib Burger

"Thick and Saucy Kansas BBQ Rib Burger"- Kansas-style barbeque: that's all you need to know, and sometimes all you want. The sweet molasses, the tangy tomato base, why wouldn't you marinade your ribs in this glorious sauce? And why wouldn't you put a slab of tender ribs between a bun? There is no answer to those questions.

Prep Time: 5 Minutes
Cook Time: 20 Minutes
Servings: 4

INGREDIENTS:

1 lb. ground pork
1 tomato, cut in fours
2 teaspoons BBQ dry rub
BBQ sauce to taste
Salt to taste
Pepper to taste
4 buns, halved

DIRECTIONS:

> Mix the ground pork with the salt, pepper and dry rub.
> Form the ground pork mixture into eight 4 ounce balls. Create each ball into a patty by using the STUFF side of the burger press to push it down.
> Fill 1 of the brisket patties with 1 quarter of the tomato.
> Place another patty on top of the stuffed patty
> Use the SEAL side of the Burger Press to keep the two patties in place. Close the press firmly, which will seal the patties together. Release the press.
> Put the patties on the grill and cook for 6 minutes on each side.
> Serve on the bun and top with the BBQ sauce.

Kentucky: Hot Brown on a Warm Bun Burger

Like Scrapple, a Hot Brown is something unfamiliar, but there's no reason why it should be. It's an open-faced sandwich consisting of turkey, bacon, and Mornay sauce. Now, it's also a burger. The Bluegrass State never fails to impress: horses, bourbon, and hot browns. It's a great recipe for racing season!

Prep Time: 5 Minutes
Cook Time: 15 Minutes
Servings: 4

INGREDIENTS:

Mornay Sauce:
¼ cup butter
¼ cup all-purpose flour
1 cup milk
2 cup chicken broth
2/2 teaspoon Worcestershire sauce
¾ cup shredded cheddar cheese
1/8 teaspoon white pepper
¼ teaspoon salt

Burger
1lb. ground turkey
8 cooked bacon strips, halved
2 medium tomatoes, sliced
1 cup shredded Parmesan cheese
Salt to taste
Pepper to taste

DIRECTIONS:

› Sauce: Melt the butter in a large saucepan on low heat.
› Stir in the flour until smooth.
› Gradually add milk, broth and Worcestershire sauce and bring to a boil.
› Cook for 2 minutes and add in the cheese, white pepper and salt.
› Remove and set aside.
› Combine the ground turkey, salt and pepper in a bowl.

> Form the ground turkey mixture into four 4 ounce balls. Create each ball into a patty by using the STUFF side of the burger press to push it down.
> Put the patties on the grill and cook for 6 minutes on each side.
> Serve on a bun and top with the tomato, bacon, Parmesan cheese, and Mornay sauce

Louisiana: Gooey Gumbo Cajun Burger

Cajun food is where it's at, and Louisiana is where to find one of America's most authentic cuisines. I greatly enjoy gumbo because it's versatile and you can use many ingredients. There's no need for Mardi Gras to celebrate the Bayou's culinary contributions, you can consume it all summer long.

Prep Time: 5 Minutes
Cook Time: 30 Minutes
Servings: 6

INGREDIENTS:

Burgers
1 lb. ground beef
1 lb. frozen shrimp, pre-cooked and pre-tailed
1 medium onion, chopped
1 can condensed Chicken Gumbo Soup
1 tablespoon yellow mustard
1/8 teaspoon ground black pepper
6 Sesame Seed buns, halved

DIRECTIONS:
> Combine the ground beef, onion, soup, mustard and black pepper together.
> Form the ground beef mixture into six 4 ounce balls. Create each ball into a patty by using the STUFF side of the burger press to push it down.
> Fill 1 of the patties with the ¼ of the shrimp in the center of each patty.
> Place the other patty on top of the other patty
> Use the SEAL side of the Burger Press to keep the two patties in place. Close the press firmly, which will seal the patties together. Release the press.
> Put the patties on the grill and cook for 6 minutes on each side.
> Serve on a bun and top with any preference of condiments.

Maine: The Big Maine Seafood Experience Burger

We can all act rich at one point in our life, right? There's nothing wrong with splurging a little and sharing with your friends and family. Lobster is good. Butter is good. Lobster butter burgers are good. Atlantic seafood is some of the freshest in the world, and one of our more ignored states certainly knows how to catch and prepare the aquatic delicacy.

Prep Time: 5
Cook Time: 10
Servings: 4

INGREDIENTS:

1 pound lumped lobster meat
4 tablespoons cubed and chilled butter
1 teaspoon lemon zest
1 teaspoon lemon juice
Salt to taste
Pepper to taste
Tartar sauce for topping
Napa cabbage for topping
Green cabbage for topping
Carrots, shaved for topping
Sliced French bread, toasted and buttered

DESCRIPTION:

> Mix the lobster meat, lemon zest, and salt and pepper together in a bowl.
> Form the lobster mixture into eight 4 ounce balls. Create each ball into a patty by using the STUFF side of the burger press to push it down.
> Fill 1 of the patties with 1 tablespoon of butter
> Place the other patty on top of the other patty
> Use the SEAL side of the Burger Press to keep the two patties in place. Close the press firmly, which will seal the patties together. Release the press.
> Fry in a pan for 6 minutes on each side.

> ❯ Serve: bottom of French bread add tartar sauce, Napa cabbage, green cabbage and carrots on top of the patty, and top with the remaining bun. Serve with a wine cooler.

Maryland: Can't Miss Crab Cake Burger

"If I may quote *Wedding Crashers*, "Crab Cakes and football, that's what Maryland does." Well, crab cakes for sure, The Redskins and Ravens need to start holding up their end of the bargain. You can make crab cakes right at home, they aren't as difficult as you would think, and then slide the tender meat between a bun to make your backyard barbeque a hit (I could have said *touchdown* there)!

Prep Time: 10 Minutes
Cook Time: 15 Minutes
Servings: 8

INGREDIENTS:

2 pounds jumbo lump crab meat
2 eggs
¾ cup mayonnaise
½ lemon, juiced
1 teaspoon Worcestershire
1 tablespoon Dijon mustard
2 teaspoons baking powder
½ cup panko
1 teaspoon crab boil seasoning
8 parsley leaves
1 tablespoon dill weed
8 servings of hamburger buns, halved

DIRECTIONS:

> Mix all the ingredients, but the parsley together.
> Form the crab cake mixture into eight 4 ounce balls. Create each ball into a patty by using the STUFF side of the burger press to push it down.
> Fill 1 of the patties with 1 parsley leaf.
> Place the other patty on top of the other patty
> Use the SEAL side of the Burger Press to keep the two patties in place. Close the press firmly, which will seal the patties together. Release the press.
> Put the patties on the grill and cook for 6 minutes on each side.
> Serve: on the bun and top with some tartar or cocktail sauce.

Massachusetts: Creamy Clam Chowder Burger

Now, if I may quote a password from *Ace Ventura*, "New England Clam Chowder." It doesn't matter if it's the red or the white, Massachusetts is known for this amazing dish. The chowder is good by itself, but a burger covered in the tasty and chunky clam soup is a great Northeastern delight that will be sure to please.

Prep Time: 5 Minutes
Cook Time: 20 Minutes
Servings: 6

INGREDIENTS:

1 lb. ground beef
1 can clams
1 medium onion, chopped
1 can condensed clam chowder
1 tablespoon whipping cream
1/8 teaspoon ground black pepper
6 Sesame Seed buns, halved

DIRECTIONS:

> Combine the ground beef, onion, soup, whipping cream and black pepper together.
> Form the ground beef mixture into twelve 4 ounce balls. Create each ball into a patty by using the STUFF side of the burger press to push it down.
> Fill 1 of the patties with a little bit of clams.
> Place the other patty on top of the other patty
> Use the SEAL side of the Burger Press to keep the two patties in place. Close the press firmly, which will seal the patties together. Release the press.
> Put the patties on the grill and cook for 6 minutes on each side.
> Serve on a toasted bun with butter.

Michigan: Stuffed Pasties Burger

"You would think a patsy is close to a pastry, but is Sheppard's Pie really close to a pie? Potato Potato (you know what I'm going for there). And yes, there are potatoes in a pasty as well as bee, and everything else that is delicious. Stuff it, put in between a bun, and enjoy!

Prep Time: 10 Minutes
Cook Time: 15 Minutes
Servings: 6

INGREDIENTS:
Stuffing ingredients:
½ cups shortening
½ cups water, boiled
3 cups all-purpose flour
1 tsp. salt

Patty:
6 large red potatoes, peeled
2 medium rutabagas, peeled
1 medium onion, chopped
1 lb. ground beef
½ lb. ground pork
¼ tbsp. salt
1 tsp. pepper
1 tsp. garlic powder

Toppings:
6 sets of buns
Mayo
Ketchup
Mustard
Cheese
Lettuce
Tomato

DIRECTIONS:

❯ Mix the shortening and water in a large bowl. It will melt.

❯ Slowly stir in flour and salt. It will form into dough.

❯ Cover and place in fridge for 1 hour

❯ Next, start making the patties. Wash, quarter, and slice the potatoes and rutabagas.

❯ Place in a bowl with the onion, beef, pork and seasonings.

❯ Form the meat mixture into twelve 4 ounce balls. Create each ball into a patty by using the STUFF side of the burger press to push it down.

❯ Fill 1 of the patties with 6 equal portions of the dough.

❯ Place the other patty on top of the other patty

❯ Use the SEAL side of the Burger Press to keep the two patties in place. Close the press firmly, which will seal the patties together. Release the press.

❯ Put the patties on the grill and cook for 6 minutes on each side.

❯ Serve: On the bun and top with all your favorite toppings and enjoy.

Minnesota: Juicy Lucy Burger

"Juicy Lucy Burger"- Juicy Lucy is actually a technique that everyone uses, they just don't know it. How many times have you stuffed your burger with cheese? A lot. That's a juicy Lucy, and we must thank our Northern residents for bringing this to the dinner table. I'm not really sure who Lucy is, but we'll give her the most credit.

Prep Time: 15 Minutes
Cook Time: 10 Minutes
Servings: 4

INGREDIENTS:

1 ½ pounds lean ground beef
1 tablespoon Worcestershire sauce
¾ teaspoon garlic salt
1 teaspoon black pepper
4 slices American cheese
4 slices provolone cheese
4 hamburger buns, halved

DIRECTIONS:

> Combine the ground beef, Worcestershire sauce, garlic salt, and black pepper into a bowl.
> Form the ground beef mixture into eight 4 ounce balls. Create each ball into a patty by using the STUFF side of the burger press to push it down.
> Fill 1 of the patties with a slice of American and provolone cheese in the center of each patty.
> Place the other patty on top of the other patty
> Use the SEAL side of the Burger Press to keep the two patties in place. Close the press firmly, which will seal the patties together. Release the press.
> Put the patties on the grill and cook for 6 minutes on each side.
> Serve on a bun and top with an onion and tomato on top of the burger patty.

Mississippi: Mississippi Mud Burger

Eeeeaks,... that doesn't sound appetizing, but it's not really mud so calm down. It's a pie! The thing I remember most about Mississippi as a child is knowing how to spell it, and now as an adult I can remember this delicious dessert burger. The South has some secrets, so don't be afraid to explore their culinary expertise!

Prep Time: 10 Minutes
Cook Time: 40 Minutes
Servings: 6

INGREDIENTS:

Mississippi Mud
Stout Mushrooms
1 lb. Crimini Mushrooms, pureed
¼ cup beef stock
1 12 ounce Lazy Magnolia Jefferson Stout
2 tablespoons olive oil
¼ shallots, minced
1 teaspoon salt
1 teaspoon pepper

Cheese Spread
½ cup cheddar cheese, grated
½ cup sour cream
3 tablespoons pimentos, pureed
¼ cup scallion tips, sliced
2 tablespoons mayonnaise
1 tablespoon chipotle sauce
1 teaspoon Worcestershire sauce

Slaw
3 cups shredded cabbage, shredded
½ cup bread and butter pickles, diced
1 tablespoon pickled jalapenos, diced
¼ cup Vidalia onion, diced

½ cup grape tomatoes, diced
1 teaspoon chipotle pepper sauce
¼ cup butter pickle juice
¼ cup mayonnaise
1 teaspoon celery seed
1 teaspoon black pepper
1 teaspoon salt

Burger
2 ¼ lb. ground beef
1 tablespoon pepper
1 tablespoon salt
1 tablespoon parsley, ground
2 tablespoons garlic, minced
6 Kaiser rolls, halved

DIRECTIONS:

> Mississippi Mud: Sauté the chopped shallots in skillet on medium heat for 1 minute.
> Add the remaining ingredients for the sauce and reduce for 10 minutes.
> Set aside and keep warm
> Cheese Spread: Pour all ingredients into a blender or food processor and blend for 1 minute.
> Set aside and chill.
> Slaw: Place the cabbage, tomatoes, onion, pickles and jalapenos to one bowl and the wet ingredients into another.
> Mix the wet ingredients until blended.
> Set aside and chill.
> Place the onions and mushrooms in a pan and cook for 20 minutes. Add the parsley and set to the side to cool.
> Burger: Combine all the ingredients in a bowl.
> Form the ground beef mixture into twelve 4 ounce balls. Create each ball into a patty by using the STUFF side of the burger press to push it down.
> Fill 1 of the patties with a little of the cheese mixture into the center of each patty.
> Place the other patty on top of the other patty
> Use the SEAL side of the Burger Press to keep the two patties in place. Close the press firmly, which will seal the patties together. Release the press.

> Put the patties on the grill and cook for 6 minutes on each side.
> Serve with the patty on the bottom bun, top with the Mississippi Mud sauce, top with the slaw, place the top piece of bun on top and enjoy.

Missouri: The Gateway to Flavorful Cheeseburger Stuffed Ravioli Burger

I know when you think Italian, you think Missouri. Okay, be honest, you think barbeque, and rightfully so, St. Louis has its own style of the American classic. However, Missouri also has its own style of the Italian classic so get cooking because you're missing out!

Prep Time: 5 Minutes
Cook Time: 20 Minutes
Servings: 4

INGREDIENTS:

Tomato Sauce:
1 large white onion, sliced
1 tablespoon butter
1 28-ouce can crushed tomatoes
1 tablespoon Worcestershire sauce
1 tablespoon oregano
Salt to taste

Ravioli:
4 ½ cups flour
6 eggs
1 tablespoon olive oil
I teaspoon salt

Burger:
1 ½ pounds ground beef
½ cup ricotta cheese
8 slices provolone cheese
Salt to taste
Pepper to taste
4 burger buns, halved

DIRECTIONS:

> Sauce: Heat the butter and onion in saucepan on medium. Sprinkle some salt.
> Sauté the onions for 20 minutes.
> Pour in the tomatoes, oregano, and Worcestershire.
> Simmer while making the rest of the recipe.
> Pasta: Pour all ingredients into a blender or food processor.
> Cover the dough with plastic wrap and refrigerate for 30 minutes.
> Roll the pasta to the third thinnest setting on the pasta roller.
> Cut the dough into large squares that will fit the burger patties.
> Burger: Mix the ground beef, salt and pepper into a bowl.
> Form the ground beef into four 4 ounce balls. Create each ball into a patty by using the STUFF side of the burger press to push it down.
> Put the patties on the grill and cook for 2 minutes on each side.
> Stuff: Take one of the squares and place 2 tablespoons of ricotta, top with the burger, and then a piece of the cheese.
> Wet the edges of the dough with your fingers to seal the pasta in place.
> Boil a pot of salted water over medium.
> Drop the ravioli in the water and simmer for 8 minutes.
> Serve: on a bun, top with the sauce and enjoy.

Montana: Mountainous Rocky Mountain Oyster Burger

It's best that your guests really aren't aware of what these are. I know what they are, and they're good, trust me, and that's all your diners need to know to enjoy this tender, juicy meat. What a strange description for bull testicles, but again, it's true! Give this delicacy a shot and you will be pleasantly surprised.

Prep Time: 5 minutes
Cook Time: 20 Minutes
Servings: 4

INGREDIENTS:
Rocky Mountain Oysters:
2 lbs. bull testicles, frozen
2 tablespoons salt
1 tablespoon vinegar
1 cup flour
¼ cup cornmeal
1cup red wine
Salt to taste
Pepper to taste
Garlic powder to taste
Bottled hot sauce
Cooking oil for frying

Burger
1½ lbs. lean ground bison
1 tablespoon salt
1 tablespoon pepper
1 tablespoon garlic powder
1 cup BBQ sauce
4 buns, halved

DIRECTIONS:

> Rocky Mountain Oysters: Start by splitting the tough muscle surrounding the oyster with a knife.
> Place the oysters in a pan of salt water and soak for 1 hour.
> Drain the oysters and pour in large pot.
> Add water to cover the meat.
> Pour the vinegar in the pot. Boil, rinse and drain.
> Let the oysters cool.
> Slice each oyster into ¼ inch ovals.
> Sprinkle them with salt and pepper.
> Mix the flour, cornmeal and garlic powder together.
> Pour milk and wine in a separate bowl and dip the oysters in the flour mixture, milk and then repeat.
> Dip the oysters in wine.
> Fry the oysters in the oil until golden brown
> Burger: Mix the ground bison, salt, pepper, BBQ sauce, and garlic powder into a bowl.
> Form the ground bison into eight 4 ounce balls. Create each ball into a patty by using the STUFF side of the burger press to push it down.
> Fill 1 of the patties with a few of the oysters.
> Place the other patty on top of the other patty
> Use the SEAL side of the Burger Press to keep the two patties in place. Close the press firmly, which will seal the patties together. Release the press.
> Put the patties on the grill and cook for 6 minutes on each side
> Serve: Put the remaining BBQ sauce on a bun and top with lettuce and tomato.

BEFORE TURNING THE NEXT PAGE...
REVIEW THE BOOK ON AMAZON

If you were please with our book then **please leave us a review on Amazon where you purchased this book!** www.amazon.com/dp/B076JDHW9Z In the world of an author who writes books independently, your reviews are not only touching but important so that we know you like the material we have prepared for "you" our audience! So leave us a review...we would love to see that you enjoyed our book!

If for any reason that you were less than happy with your experience then send me an email at **Feedback@Healthylifestylerecipes.org** and let me know how we can better your experience. We always come out with a few volumes of our books and will possibly be able to address some of your concerns. Do keep in mind that we strive to do our best to give you the highest quality of what "we the independent authors" pour our heart and tears into.

I am very happy to create new and exciting recipes and do appreciate your purchase. I thank you for your many great reviews and comments! With a warm heart! ~"Professional Chef and Burger Experts" Richard Erwin and Tasha :)

Nebraska: The Ultimate Original Tangy Ruben Burger

"The Ultimate Original Rueben Burger"- If I was a betting man, I would have been certain that the famous Rueben was conjured in a New York kitchen. It wasn't! The forgotten Midwestern state takes credit for providing us with one of the great American sandwiches. Good thing I don't gamble, Nebraska would easily have been in the bottom 10 ranking of where I thought the Rueben was created.

Prep Time: 15 Minutes
Cook Time: 20 Minutes
Servings: 4

INGREDIENTS:

Dressing:
½ cup mayonnaise
¼ cup ketchup
¼ cup pickle relish
1 tablespoon rice wine vinegar
1 teaspoon celery seed
1 teaspoon Tabasco
2 cups sauerkraut, drained

Burger:
1 pound ground beef
1 pound ground corned beef
1 pound ground pork
1 cup sauerkraut, drained
4 slices Swiss cheese
Salt to taste
Pepper to taste
4 Kaiser Rolls, halved

DIRECTIONS:

> Dressing: Mix all of the ingredients together and set aside
> Combine the corned beef, ground beef, ground pork, salt and pepper in a bowl.
> Form the ground mixture into eight 4 ounce balls. Create each ball into a patty by using the STUFF side of the burger press to push it down.
> Fill 1 of the patties with a ¼ of the sauerkraut.
> Place the other patty on top of the other patty
> Use the SEAL side of the Burger Press to keep the two patties in place. Close the press firmly, which will seal the patties together. Release the press.
> Put the patties on the grill and cook for 6 minutes on each side
> Serve: Put the dressing on a bun and top with lettuce and tomato.

Nevada: All-You-Can-Eat Jackpot Burger

"All-You-Can-Eat Jackpot Burger"- As mentioned in Nebraska, good thing I don't gamble or I would be in trouble if I went to Las Vegas without other intentions to eat. Well, let's just say what happens to this author stays with this author. Vegas buffets aren't your regular discount Chinese or comfort food joints; they have everything and it's quality. That's why it's so expensive, but you can just go and win your money to afford to eat. Or you can put everything in a burger in your backyard.

Prep Time: 5 Minutes
Cook Time: 20 Minutes
Servings: 4

INGREDIENTS:
Slaw:
½ head of red Napa cabbage, shaved
½ head of green cabbage, shaved
½ cup carrots, shaved
½ cup red onion, diced

1 cup mayonnaise
1 tablespoon finely chopped onion
1 tablespoon ketchup
1 teaspoon prepared mustard
1/4 teaspoon salt
 1/8 teaspoon pepper
1 pound lean ground beef (90% lean)
½ pound bacon, chopped
1 avocado, quartered
1 frozen bag of onion rings, cooked
1/4 cup finely shredded cheddar cheese
 4 hamburger buns, halved
Lettuce leaves, pickles and tomato slices, optional

DIRECTIONS:

> Slaw: Mix all the slaw ingredients together and set aside.
> Combine the onion, ketchup, mustard, salt and pepper in a bowl. Mix these ingredients with the beef.
> Form the ground beef mixture into eight 4 ounce balls. Create each ball into a patty by using the STUFF side of the burger press to push it down.
> Fill 1 of the patties with a handful of cheese, bacon, and onion rings in the center of each patty.
> Place the other patty on top of the other patty
> Use the SEAL side of the Burger Press to keep the two patties in place. Close the press firmly, which will seal the patties together. Release the press.
> Put the patties on the grill and cook for 6 minutes on each side.
> Serve: on buns with thousand island, lettuce, pickle and tomato if desired. Top the onion ring on top of the bun with a toothpick.

New Hampshire: Tangy Crisp Apple Stuffed Pork burgers

People don't use fruit enough with meat. Here's a little secret for you: when slow-cooking beef ribs, I lay slices of pear around the rack for a subtle sweetness. It's delicious, and when done, the pear is tasty drenched in barbeque sauce. The same goes with apples, especially from New Hampshire. Either slice them and lay them on top the patty, or use the juice to cook with!

Prep Time: 5 Minutes
Cook Time: 30 Minutes
Servings: 8

INGREDIENTS:

1 pound ground pork
2 medium Granny Smith apples, grated
2 tablespoons fresh Italian parsley, chopped
1 teaspoon fresh rosemary, chopped
1 teaspoon salt
¼ teaspoon fresh ground pepper
4 wheat buns, halved

DIRECTIONS:

> Combine the ground pork, Italian parsley, rosemary, salt and pepper into a bowl.
> Form the ground pork mixture into eight 4 ounce balls. Create each ball into a patty by using the STUFF side of the burger press to push it down.
> Fill 1 of the patties with ¼ of the apple mixture in the center of each patty.
> Place the other patty on top of the other patty
> Use the SEAL side of the Burger Press to keep the two patties in place. Close the press firmly, which will seal the patties together. Release the press.
> Put the patties on the grill and cook for 6 minutes on each side.
> Serve on a bun and top with all of the leftover apple, sprinkle with some cinnamon or nutmeg.

New Jersey: Juicy Jersey Shore Pork Roll Burger

New Jersey isn't just the Shore and *The Sopranos*. It's a vibrant state, and despite what New Yorkers think, it doesn't smell like trash. It also has a versatile cuisine, and their claim to fame is the pork roll. Add some egg and cheese atop a chop and you have yourself a great pork roll burger!

Prep Time: 5 Minutes
Cook Time: 20 Minutes
Servings: 4

INGREDIENTS:

Burger:
2 pounds ground beef
2 tablespoons ice water
1 tablespoon Worcestershire sauce
1 ½ teaspoons salt

Sauce:
½ cup ketchup
6 tablespoons Dijon mustard
2 teaspoons honey
1 teaspoon chili garlic sauce

1 tablespoon butter
6 large eggs
Salt to taste
Pepper to taste
6 thick slices Pork Roll
6 pieces American cheese
6 Kaiser Rolls, halved

DIRECTIONS:

> Sauce: mix together the mustard, ketchup, honey and chili sauce. Cover and set aside.
> Burger: Combine the ground beef, ice water, Worcestershire sauce, and salt in a mixing bowl.

> Form the ground beef into six 4 ounce balls. Create each ball into a patty by using the STUFF side of the burger press to push it down.
> Put the patties on the grill and cook for 6 minutes on each side
> Pork Roll: Place each slice of pork roll on the grill and cook for 1 minute on each side.
> Place a piece of cheese on each roll and let melt. Let cook for additional minute on the edge of the grill if you want toasted
> Egg: In a skillet, melt the butter and then add the eggs one at time.
> When the egg whites have set, break the yolks, flip the eggs and cook until done
> Serve: On the bottom part of the roll, add the sauce, patty, egg and pork slice with cheese. Top with the other half of the roll and enjoy.

New Mexico: Classic Fiery Green Chile Cheeseburger

"Classic Spicy Green Chile Cheeseburger"- New Mexican food is not Mexican food; it's actually a combination of Mexican and Native-American cuisines, with the added southwest treasure: green Chile. It's not chili dyed green, it's a spicy pepper native to the land. Warning: If you've never had New Mexican food, you may become addicted and constantly crave the style. No, really, you will be having green Chile shipped to wherever you live

Prep Time: 35 Minutes
Cook Time: 30 Minutes
Servings: 4

INGREDIENTS:

Cheese Sauce:
1 tablespoon unsalted butter
2 tablespoon all-purpose flour
1 cup whole milk
12 ounces Monterey Jack Cheese, grated
¼ cup Parmesan cheese, grated
Salt to taste
Pepper to taste

Relish:
1 medium poblano Chile, roasted, peeled, seeded and sliced
2 Hatch chilies, roasted, peeled, seeded and sliced
1 Serrano Chile, roasted, peeled, seeded and sliced
¼ cup red wine vinegar
1 ½ tablespoon honey
2 tablespoons olive oil
2 tablespoons fresh cilantro leaves, chopped
Salt to taste
Pepper to taste

Red Onion:
1 ½ cups red wine vinegar
¼ cup water
2 tablespoons sugar
1 tablespoon salt
1 medium red onion, peeled, halved and sliced
1 tablespoon canola oil

1 ½ pounds ground beef
2 teaspoons taco seasoning
Salt to taste
Pepper to taste
4 hamburger buns, halved
12 blue corn tortilla chips, crushed
1 pound ground buffalo

DIRECTIONS:
> Cheese sauce: In a saucepan mix in the flour and cook for 1 minute on medium.
> Combine the milk, change the heat setting to high, and whisk until thick for 5 minutes.
> Take off the stove and cook until all cheese is melted. Add in the salt and pepper and set aside.
> Relish: Mix all ingredients in a bowl and set aside.
> Onion: In a small saucepan boil the vinegar, water, sugar and salt on medium heat.
> Remove from the stove and let cool for 10 minutes.
> Pour the vinegar over the onions in a medium sized bowl, cover and refrigerate for 4 hours.
> Combine ground beef, taco seasoning, salt and pepper together in a bowl
> Form the ground beef mixture into eight 4 ounce balls. Create each ball into a patty by using the STUFF side of the burger press to push it down.
> Fill 1 of the patties with ¼ of the cheese sauce.
> Place the other patty on top of the other patty
> Use the SEAL side of the Burger Press to keep the two patties in place. Close the press firmly, which will seal the patties together. Release the press.
> Put the patties on the grill and cook for 6 minutes on each side.
> Serve on a bun with relish, onions and chips.

New York: Saucy and Tangy Buffalo Wing Burger

New York is tough because the city is so cultured and there are so many culinary influences, so we're moving over to the rest of the state that people forget exists. Buffalo: where wings became way too delicious. Butter and hot sauce is a classic combination, and to drench a chicken breast and place in between a bun is just smart.

Prep Time: 5 Minutes
Cook Time: 10 Minutes
Servings: 8

INGREDIENTS:

2 pounds ground beef
5 ounces blue cheese, crumbled
1/3 cup mayonnaise
¼ cup sour cream
½ teaspoon red wine vinegar
½ cup Frank's Red Hot Sauce
3 tablespoons unsalted butter, melted and cooled
1 teaspoon honey
1 cup thick blue cheese dressing
8 hamburger buns, halved

DIRECTIONS:

> Combine the cheese, mayonnaise, sour cream and vinegar into a bowl.
> In a separate bowl combine the hot sauce, butter and honey.
> Form the ground beef into four eight ounce balls. Create each ball into a patty by using the STUFF side of the burger press to push it down.
> Put the patties on the grill and cook for 6 minutes on each side.
> Spread the blue cheese mixture on the bottom of the bun, top with a burger, add some hit sauce and dressing top and add the top bun. Serve the celery, carrots and remaining blue cheese dressing on the side.

North Carolina: Simmering Tender Pulled Pork Burger

"Simmering Tender Pulled Pork Burger"- Another barbeque haven, North Carolina is on top of the game when it comes to marinating and cooking meat. Their specialty: pulled pork. Your new specialty: a pulled pork burger. Either put the tender meat between a bun, or add it to the top of a beef patty and smother in barbeque sauce. Don't deny it, you thought about it.

Prep Time: 15 Minutes
Cook Time: 15 Minutes
Servings: 4

INGREDIENTS:
1 pound ground beef
Salt to taste
Pepper to taste

Toppings:
4 slices American cheese
1 1/3 cup deli coleslaw
1 cup pulled pork with BBQ sauce, warmed
½ French fried onions
4 potato hamburger buns, halved

DIRECTIONS:
> Combine the ground beef, salt and pepper into a bowl.
> Form the ground beef into eight 4 ounce balls. Create each ball into a patty by using the STUFF side of the burger press to push it down.
> Put the patties on the grill and cook for 6 minutes on each side
> Serve: pour 1/3 of the coleslaw on the bottom half of each bun. Top with a patty, ¼ of the pulled pork, 2 tablespoons French fried onions and top with the other half of the bun.

North Dakota: Roaming Big Bison Burger

North Dakota is an overlooked state, but it shouldn't be; it's just when traveling North you always stop in South Dakota and think that's enough Dakota for one trip. With that being said, Bison is an overlooked meat, but it shouldn't be. It's lean, it's delicious, and sometimes can transform an ordinary burger into an extraordinary one.

Prep Time: 15 Minutes
Cook Time: 6 Minutes
Servings: 4

INGREDIENTS:

Burger:
1 pound ground bison
1 pound ground beef
1 yellow onion, minced
4 cloves garlic, minced
2 tablespoons fresh parsley, chopped
1 tablespoon onion powder
1 tablespoon garlic powder
1 teaspoon seasoning salt
¼ cup ketchup
2 tablespoons Worcestershire Sauce
Pepper to taste
Salt to taste
4 slices Wisconsin Cheddar Cheese
1 cup fresh arugula greens
4 pickle slices
4 hamburger buns, halved

Mayonnaise Spread:
½ cup mayonnaise
2 tablespoons fresh parsley, chopped
4 raw garlic cloves, chopped
Salt to taste
Pepper to taste

DIRECTIONS:

>   Mayonnaise spread: Combine all the ingredients in a bowl and set aside.
>   Mix the ground bison, ground bison, onions, garlic and parsley in a bowl. Add in the onion powder, garlic powder, seasoning salt, ketchup, Worcestershire, pepper and salt together.
>   Form the ground bison mixture into eight 4 ounce balls. Create each ball into a patty by using the STUFF side of the burger press to push it down.
>   Fill 1 of the pork patties with 1 slice of the Wisconsin Cheddar Cheese.
>   Place one patty on top of the filled patty.
>   Use the SEAL side of the Burger Press to keep the two patties in place. Close the press firmly, which will seal the patties together. Release the press.
>   Put the patties on the grill and cook for 6 minutes on each side.
>   Serve: Spread the mayo on the bottom half of the bun, place the burger on top, then cover with arugula, top with the other half of the bun and add the pickle on top of the bun with a toothpick.

Ohio: Chunky Cheesy Chili Burger

"Chunky Chili Burger"- Though Ohio is a pretty small state land wise, it has so much to offer. Whenever you hear of a famous person, they have Ohio roots, or whenever you hear of something great, it originated in Ohio. All they get from this book is the chili. Even Wendy's has great chili – the franchise started in Ohio if you were wondering why I said that. They don't put it on a burger though, so get on it!

Prep Time: 10 Minutes
Cook Time: 15 Minutes
Servings: 4

INGREDIENTS:

12 onion rings, cooked
1 ½ pounds ground beef
Salt to taste
Pepper to taste
4 slices yellow cheddar cheese
1 cup prepared chili, warmed
1/3 cup BBQ sauce
4 brioche buns, halved

DIRECTIONS:

> Combine the ground beef, salt and pepper together.
> Form the ground beef mixture into four 4 ounce balls. Create each ball into a patty by using the STUFF side of the burger press to push it down.
> Put the patties on the grill and cook for 6 minutes on each side. Add a cheese slice on the last minute of grilling.
> Serve: Place the patty on the bottom bun, chili, onion rings, BBQ sauce and cover with the top bun.

Oklahoma: Gravy-drenched Chicken Fried Steak Burger

Gravy, chicken-fried steak, and burgers are as American as Oklahoma. I literally could leave it at that, but I must reiterate how classic of a meal this is, and though it's usually made for you to overeat and feel guilty afterwards, you can control the portions in burger form in your backyard!

Prep Time: 5 Minutes
Cook Time: 20 Minutes
Servings: 4

INGREDIENTS:

1½ lbs. ground beef
½ cup all-purpose flour
1 tablespoon cornstarch
½ teaspoon salt
¼ teaspoon freshly ground black pepper
1/8 teaspoon cayenne pepper
1 teaspoon garlic powder
2 tablespoons unsalted butter
1 large sweet onion, sliced thinly1 cup beef stock
½ cup whole milk
4 large onion rolls, halved
1 jar French fried onions

DIRECTIONS:

> Mix the flour, cornstarch, and all the seasonings in a bowl.
> Place 3 tablespoons of the mixture into another bowl and set aside.
> Combine the ground beef with the first flour mixture.
> Form the ground beef into four 4 ounce balls. Create each ball into a patty by using the STUFF side of the burger press to push it down.
> Put the patties on the grill and cook for 6 minutes on each side.
> Gravy: Cook the onions in a medium sized pan for 7 minutes.
> Add the leftover flour fix, stir and cook for 1 minute.
> Pour in the broth, and milk.

> Increase the heat and stir to prevent lumps from forming.
> Bring to a bowl and deglaze the bottom of the pan to release any brown bits sticking to the pan.
> Reduce the heat to low, add the patties and simmer for 15 minutes.
> Serve: Put the chicken fried patty on the bottom half of the roll, top with gravy, and French friend onions. Top with the top half of the bun and enjoy.

Oregon: Sweet and Tart Marionberry Dessert Burger

Sweet meat: it's been done before, however, sometimes even a burger can be meatless. They have dessert pizza, so why not dessert burgers? Oregon is known for weird people, and weird people are known for great pies – them and country grandmothers. Here's a spin on one the Pacific Northwest's best fruits.

Prep Time: 5 Minutes
Cook Time: 20 Minutes
Servings: 6

INGREDIENTS:

2 cans of ground salmon
2 garlic cloves, chopped
2 green onions, chopped
½ teaspoon lemon zest
½ teaspoon thyme, chopped
1/2 teaspoon black pepper
1 teaspoon coarse salt
2 egg yolks
¼ cup mayonnaise
¼ cup bread crumbs
1 teaspoon olive oil
1 red onion, sliced
1 head of leaf lettuce
6 Kaiser Rolls, halved
1 cup BBQ sauce, store bought
1 pint Marionberries
8 oz. cream cheese, softened
¼ half and half
¼ teaspoon lemon zest
½ teaspoon lemon juice

DIRECTIONS:

> Sauce: Combine the BBQ sauce and Marionberries in a saucepan and cook on medium heat. Cook until it is consistent.
> Add the cream cheese, lemon zest and juice together in a bowl and stir until it reaches creamy texture.
> Mix the ground salmon, garlic, green onion, lemon zest, thyme, pepper, salt, egg yolks, mayo, bread crumbs and olive oil.
> Form the ground salmon mixture into four 4 ounce balls. Create each ball into a patty by using the STUFF side of the burger press to push it down.
> Put the patties on the grill and cook for 6 minutes on each side. Spread some of the Marion berry sauce on the patties the last minute of grilling.
> Serve: Place a salmon patty on top of a bottom bun; add Marion berry sauce, lettuce and onion slices. Spread the cream cheese mixture on the top bun and place on the burger. Enjoy.

Pennsylvania: Loaded Creamy Cheesesteak Burgers

I'm a sucker for cheesesteaks, and I'm lactose intolerant: that's how much I love them. Thanks to the great people at Lactaid. You can keep this classic in a hoagie or move it to a bun, but homemade cheesesteaks are a possibility if you can't make it to Geno's on a whim.

Prep Time: 15 Minutes
Cook Time: 15 Minutes
Servings: 4

INGREDIENTS:

Cheesesteak:
2 tablespoons canola oil
1 green bell pepper, sliced
½ yellow onion, sliced
1 pound ribeye steak, thinly sliced
1 tablespoon Worcestershire Sauce
Salt to taste
Pepper to taste

Burger:
1 pound lean ground beef
½ cup mayonnaise
4 slices provolone cheese
4 brioche buns, halved

DIRECTIONS

> Cheesesteak: Combine the bell pepper, onions and oil in a bowl.
> Cook the mixture in a pan on high heat until crispy,
> Remove the vegetable mixture and add the steak, searing on both sides.
> Form the ground beef mixture into four 4 ounce balls. Create each ball into a patty by using the STUFF side of the burger press to push it down.
> Put the patties on the grill and cook for 6 minutes on each side. Add the provolone cheese to the patties during the second half of cooking.

❯ Serve: Spread mayonnaise on both sides of the bun; add lettuce, patty (cheese side up), a portion of the steak, and vegetables. Enjoy.

Rhode Island: Refreshing Island Breeze Lemonade Burger

Rhode Island remains a state, and if I may quote a Mike Myers SNL skit, "Rhode Island: neither a road nor an island. Talk amongst yourselves." It is, however, a great place for frozen lemonade and relaxing. You can incorporate lemon into your burger in many ways: marinade, zest, sliced, whatever! It's definitely a tangy twist.

Prep Time: 5 Minutes
Cook Time: 20 Minutes
Servings: 4

INGREDIENTS:
1 pound ground beef
2 tablespoons lemon juice
1 teaspoon lemon zest
1 tablespoon fresh parsley, chopped
¾ teaspoon salt
1/8 teaspoon pepper
4 buns, halved

DIRECTIONS:
> Combine all burger ingredients into a bowl.
> Form the mixture into six 4 ounce balls. Create each ball into a patty by using the STUFF side of the burger press to push it down.
> Put the patties on the grill and cook for 6 minutes on each side
> Serve on a bun with lettuce, tomato, and other toppings you like.

South Carolina: Classic Hearty Carolina Shrimp and Grits Burger

The North (Carolina) has great pulled pork while the South (Carolina) has great grits. Grits are a Southern staple, but South Carolina owns Shrimp and Grits. The flavors balance each other out and make a perfect addition to a burger. Maybe it's time these Carolinas came together.

Prep Time: 5 Minutes
Cook Time: 20 Minutes
Servings: 4

INGREDIENTS:

Grits:
2 cups regular grits
6 cups chicken stock
Parchment paper
Vegetable oil cooking spray
1 /2 tablespoons unsalted butter
½ cup grated Parmesan

Sauce:
2 tablespoons butter
3 tablespoons all-purpose flour
1 tablespoon garlic
1 scallion, minced
½ cup clam juice
½ cup water
½ cup heavy cream
1 teaspoon Worcestershire sauce
1 teaspoon hot sauce

1 pound of ground chicken
1 pound of ground shrimp
Kosher Salt
Fresh Ground Peppers
½ cup of lemon juice

4 hamburger buns, halved

DIRECTIONS:

> Grits: Make the grits according to package directions.
> Line parchment paper on a baking sheet and coat with cooking spray.
> Stir the Parmesan, butter and salt and pepper into the grits.
> Pour the grits evenly onto the sheet.
> Cover and chill for 2 ½ hours.
> Use a round cookie cutter to cut out 8 cakes.
> Sauce: Melt butter into a saucepan. Add the scallions, and garlic. Stir and cook for 2 minutes.
> Add the flour to the pan and mix with the butter, scallions and garlic. Cook for another two minutes.
> Pour in the clam juice and stir slowly.
> Next, pour in the cream, hot sauce, and Worcestershire sauce.
> Burger: Mix the ground chicken and ground shrimp with the salt and pepper and lemon juice
> Form the ground chicken mixture and the ground shrimp mixture into eight 4 ounce balls. Create each ball into a patty by using the STUFF side of the burger press to push it down.
> Fill 1 of the chicken patties with one of the grit patties.
> Place one patty on top of the other patty
> Use the SEAL side of the Burger Press to keep the two patties in place. Close the press firmly, which will seal the patties together. Release the press.
> Put the patties on the grill and cook for 6 minutes on each side.
> Serve: Place the patty on top of the bottom bun, drizzle with sauce and top with cheese.

South Dakota: Delicious Deep Fried Beef Tip Burger

South Dakota's specific culinary expertise is Chislic: another crazy American dish that people need to be more aware of. Essentially it is deep-friend beef tips, but if you take it off a stick and put it between a bun then you have yourself a delicious take on another American classic.

Prep Time: 5 Minutes
Cook Time: 10 Minutes
Servings: 4

INGREDIENTS:

Beef Tip:
1 pound beef tips
1 cup all-purpose flour
1 teaspoon seasoned salt
1 teaspoon black pepper
1 teaspoon salt
½ cup canola oil
2 tablespoons butter

1 tablespoon finely chopped onion
1 tablespoon ketchup
1 teaspoon prepared mustard
1/4 teaspoon salt
1/8 teaspoon pepper
1 pound lean ground beef (90% lean)
¼ cup finely shredded cheddar cheese
4 hamburger buns split
Lettuce leaves and tomato slices, optional

DIRECTIONS:

> Beef Tip: In a large skillet, heat oil over medium heat.
> Combine the flour, seasoned salt and pepper.
> Season the beef tips with salt and pepper.

> Cover the tips in the flour mixture.
> Add the butter in the pan before frying.
> When melted, fry the tips for one side and flip when golden brown.
> Remove and set aside.
> Burger: Combine the onion, ketchup, mustard, salt and pepper in a bowl. Mix these ingredients with the beef mixture.
> Form the ground beef mixture into four 4 ounce balls. Create each ball into a patty by using the STUFF side of the burger press to push it down.
> Fill 1 of the patties with a handful of cheese in the center of each patty.
> Place the other patty on top of the other patty
> Use the SEAL side of the Burger Press to keep the two patties in place. Close the press firmly, which will seal the patties together. Release the press.
> Put the patties on the grill and cook for 6 minutes on each side.
> Serve: on buns with lettuce, tomato and BBQ sauce if desired.

Tennessee: Smoky Mountain Whiskey-Braised Rib Burger

Does anyone else think it's weird that Tennessee is known for whiskey when many of their counties are dry? As long as they keep producing quality alcohol it doesn't matter. Whiskey is great to cook with as well, mixing the liquor with barbeque sauce is undeniably delicious, and then spreading it over a rack of ribs brings out that model smoky flavor.

Prep Time: 15 Minutes
Cook Time: 10 Minutes
Servings: 2

INGREDIENTS:

1 tablespoon unsalted butter
1 onion, sliced
1 apple, diced
1 ½ teaspoons salt
1 ½ teaspoons pepper
2 tablespoons whiskey
1 pound ground beef
½ teaspoon ground cumin
½ teaspoon chili powder
2 tablespoons blue cheese crumbles
2 sesame hamburger buns, halved

DIRECTIONS:

> Melt the butter in a sauté pan on low heat. Add the onion to the pan and cook for 10 minutes.
> Pour in the apples, salt and pepper to the pan and cook for another 10 minutes.
> Deglaze the pan with Whiskey. Remove and set aside.
> Mix the ground beef with the salt, pepper, cumin and chili powder.
> Form the ground beef mixture into eight 4 ounce balls. Create each ball into a patty by using the STUFF side of the burger press to push it down.
> Fill 1 of the patties with ¼ of the onion mixture.

> ❭ Place the other patty on top of the other patty
> ❭ Use the SEAL side of the Burger Press to keep the two patties in place. Close the press firmly, which will seal the patties together. Release the press.
> ❭ Put the patties on the grill and cook for 6 minutes on each side.
> ❭ Serve on the bun the blue cheese crumbles.

Texas: Marinated Smoked Texas Rodeo Round Up Brisket Burger

Everything is bigger in Texas, so bring your backyard appetite. You really can't go wrong with any meat from the Lone Star State, but personally I think brisket is the best choice. Smoky, saucy, and slow-cooked, and then put in a bun or on a burger is just tops. Cowboy hat optional.

Prep Time: 20 Minutes
Cook Time: 15 minutes
Servings: 4

INGREDIENTS:

1 pound ground brisket
1 teaspoon salt
½ teaspoon pepper
1 onion, sliced
Port cheese spread, for serving
Arugula, for serving
4 hamburger buns, halved

Mayonnaise:
Mayonnaise
Sun-dried tomatoes
Chives

DIRECTIONS:

> Combine the ground brisket with salt and pepper.
> Form the burger mixture into four 4 ounce balls. Create each ball into a patty by using the STUFF side of the burger press to push it down.
> Grill burgers for 6 minutes on each side
> Serve: top the bottom bun with the burger, port cheese, bacon, onions, arugula, and mayonnaise spread.

Utah: Death by Potato Burger

Utah has this casserole called Funeral Potatoes. I'm up in the air about the name, but people claim the cliché argument that *they're to die for*. Okay, sold. Butter, cheese, more butter, creamy chicken soup, more butter, sour cream, and more butter. I would watch your portions or the name may ring true, however, it could be worth the risk.

Prep Time: 5 Minutes
Cook Time: 20 Minutes
Servings: 8

INGREDIENTS:

Funeral potatoes:
2 12 ounce hash brown potatoes, thawed
2 cups sour cream
1 can cream of chicken soup
½ cup butter, melted
1 teaspoon salt
1 teaspoon onion powder
2 cups cheddar cheese, shredded
3 cups corn flakes, crush mixed with ½ cup melted butter

3 pounds ground beef
3 tbsp. kosher salt
3 tbsp. pepper
½ cup grated yellow onion
4 Colby Jack slices
8 hamburger patties, halved

DIRECTIONS:

> Funeral potatoes: Mix sour cream, soup and butter in a bowl.
> Add salt, onion, and cheese to the mixture.
> Add the thawed potatoes to the mixture.
> Pour in 9x13 pan and sprinkle on the cornflakes.
> Bake uncovered for 40 minutes at 350.

> Burger: Combine the ground beef, salt, pepper, and yellow onion in a small bowl.
> Form the ground beef mixture into sixteen 4 ounce balls. Create each ball into a patty by using the STUFF side of the burger press to push it down.
> Fill 1 of the patties with a slice of cheese in the center of each patty.
> Place the other patty on top of the other patty
> Use the SEAL side of the Burger Press to keep the two patties in place. Close the press firmly, which will seal the patties together. Release the press.
> Serve: place each patty on a bun, top with some of the funeral potatoes, and top with ketchup and hot sauce.

Vermont: Maple Glazed Sweet and Savory Burger

Let's face it: Vermont is essentially Canada in the United States. Therefore, their maple is completely legit. Maple is delicious on pork, but a nice glaze can sweeten up any meat. The getaway state is more than just Bed and Breakfasts; it also gives you a great burger recipe!

Prep Time: 5 Minutes
Cook Time: 20 Minutes
Servings: 4

INGREDIENTS:

1 pound ground beef
¼ cup beer
2 tablespoons Worcestershire sauce
1 -1/2 tablespoons pure maple syrup
Pepper to taste
4 slices cheddar cheese
8 slices maple bacon, cooked
4 hamburger buns, halved

DIRECTIONS

> Combine the ground beef, beef, Worcestershire, maple syrup, and pepper together.
> Form the ground beef mixture into four 4 ounce balls. Create each ball into a patty by using the STUFF side of the burger press to push it down.
> Grill for 6 minutes on each side. Add the cheese slice when the burger has 1 minute left to cook.
> Serve: place the burger on top of the bun and top with cooked bacon.

Virginia: Honey-glazed Ham for Burger

Virginia is for lovers. It has to be to balance out the craziness in that region (*cough, cough*, the government). The residents also love their food and make a mean honey-glazed ham. I know; *mean* isn't generally used when talking about lovers. The recipe is willing to kindly be shared if you're ready to expand your burger repertoire.

Prep Time: 5 Minutes
Cook Time: 10 Minutes
Servings: 4

INGREDIENTS:

Honey glaze:
1 cup honey
I cup cayenne pepper
1 cup mayonnaise

Burger:
1 pound ground pork
I tablespoon seasoning salt
Salt to taste
Pepper to taste
4 slices of American cheese
Lettuce, for serving
Tomatoes, sliced for serving
8 strips Applewood smoked bacon, cooked
4 hamburger buns, halved

DIRECTIONS:

- ❭ Honey glaze: Mix the honey, cayenne, and mayonnaise together. Set aside
- ❭ Combine the ground beef, seasoning salt, pepper and salt into a bowl.
- ❭ Form the ground beef mixture into four 4 ounce balls. Create each ball into a patty by using the STUFF side of the burger press to push it down.
- ❭ Put the patties on the grill and cook for 6 minutes on each side.
- ❭ Serve: on the bottom bun start with the lettuce, patty, honey glaze, tomato and bacon.

Washington: Thick Seared Tuna Steak Burger

The Pacific Northwest does two things very well: Grunge music and Seafood. Since I'm sure other people than 90s' rockers are reading this, we will focus on the matter at hand, specifically tuna. Tuna steaks are great and quick to make; just a little seasoning and searing on each side and you're essentially done – then you can get back to the music.

Prep Time: 5 Minutes
Cook Time: 20 Minutes
Servings: 2

INGREDIENTS:

2 ¾ inch thick tuna steaks
2 teaspoons olive oil
1 tablespoon fresh ginger, minced
2 garlic clove, minced
4 tablespoons mayonnaise
1 tablespoon fresh lemon juice
2 sesame- seed sandwich rolls
1 bunch, arugula, stems trimmed

DIRECTIONS:

> Mayonnaise: Heat olive oil in a medium skillet on high heat. Add the ginger and garlic.
> Stir for 30 seconds.
> Pour in a small bowl and mix with lemon juice. Mayonnaise, salt and pepper.
> Burgers: Put the steaks on the grill and cook for 6 minutes on each side
> Serve: Spread mayonnaise spread on the bottom half of the roll. Top with tuna, and arugula.

West Virginia: Backcountry Salted Pepperoni Roll Burger

"Backcountry Salted Pepperoni Roll Burger"- Not many other states are overlooked quite like West Virginia, but it's a beautiful country. With that being said, no one really knows what goes on there except that there may be some mountain people roaming the hills. No matter what, they make a great Pepperoni roll, proving that the salty delicacy can go on something other than a pizza – like a burger!

Prep Time: 5 Minutes
Cook Time: 20 Minutes
Servings: 4

INGREDIENTS:

Pepperoni Roll:
2 teaspoons olive oil
1 pound pizza dough
1 18 ounce package provolone cheese
1 14 ounce package pork pepperoni
2 tablespoons Parmigiano-Reggiano, grated

Burger:
1½ lbs. lean ground salami
Kosher Salt
Fresh Ground Pepper
½ cup Italian dressing
1 teaspoon garlic powder
½ teaspoon dried basil or oregano, crushed
4 slices Mozzarella and Provolone
8 artichoke hearts
Capers, for taste
1 tomato, sliced
Peppercini's. Diced
4 Romaine hearts
4 ciabatta buns, halved

DIRECTIONS:

> Pizza roll: Set the oven to 400 degrees.
> Brush a 9-inch round cake pan with olive oil and set aside.
> Roll the dough out on a floured surface and cover the provolone and the pepperoni slices.
> Roll the dough up like a jelly roll.
> Cut the roll tin to 1 inch thick slices.
> Arrange on the pan and sprinkle with the Parmesan.
> Bake for 25 minutes and set aside.
> Burger: Mix the ground salami, salt, pepper, ¼ Italian dressing, and garlic powder into a bowl.
> Form the ground salami into eight 4 ounce balls. Create each ball into a patty by using the STUFF side of the burger press to push it down.
> Fill 1 of the patties with 2 artichoke hearts and one piece of provolone and mozzarella cheese.
> Place the other patty on top of the other patty
> Use the SEAL side of the Burger Press to keep the two patties in place. Close the press firmly, which will seal the patties together. Release the press.
> Brush the patties with Italian dressing on both sides
> Put the patties on the grill and cook for 6 minutes on each side. Put some more of the dressing on the patties before they are done cooking.
> Serve: Dust the top of the roll with the dressing, and top with capers, Peppercini's, the patty and a romaine heart. Top with the pizza roll and the top of the ciabatta roll to finish the burger.

Wisconsin: Creamy Beer-Battered Cheese Curd Burger

Duh! If you thought anything other than cheese for Wisconsin then you need to read a different book. Beer was also an acceptable answer. How about beer-battered cheese curds? How about putting that on a burger? Now we're talking. That's an American meal if I've ever heard of one.

Prep Time: 20
Cook Time: 30
Servings: 4

INGREDIENTS:

Cheese Curds:
2 quarts corn oil for frying
¼ cup milk
1 cup all-purpose flour
¾ cup beer
½ teaspoon salt
2 eggs
2 pounds cheese curds tore apart

Burger:
1 ½ pounds ground beef
Salt to taste
Pepper to taste
8 slices deli ham
4 slices ice burg lettuce
4 pretzel buns, halved
Ketchup, for serving

DIRECTIONS:

> Cheese Curds: In a large saucepan, heat corn oil to 375 degrees.
> Mix together milk, flour, beer, salt, eggs to make a batter.
> Place 6 cheese curds at a time in the batter to coat.
> Fry in the pan for 2 minutes. Set aside.

> Burger: Combine beef, salt and pepper into a bowl.
> Form the ground pork into eight 4 ounce balls. Create each ball into a patty by using the STUFF side of the burger press to push it down.
> Fill 1 of the patties with 2 slices of deli ham.
> Place the other patty on top of the other patty
> Use the SEAL side of the Burger Press to keep the two patties in place. Close the press firmly, which will seal the patties together. Release the press.
> Put the patties on the grill and cook for 6 minutes on each side
> Serve: place 1 lettuce leaf on top of the bottom bun, tope with the patty, cheese curds and ketchup on the top bun.

Wyoming: Big Cowboy Juicy Jerky Burger

Steak is too easy in Wyoming. Just walk down the street anywhere at any time and you can get a quality steak. What about some jerky? Same rules apply, but it's a very unique alternative for a burger. Some salty jerky strips can be a great addition to a burger, or you can just tear off some bits and stuff the patty before grilling. Or both! You want to be a cowboy and not just intimidated by them, right?

Prep Time: 15 Minutes
Cook Time: 15 Minutes
Servings: 4

INGREDIENTS:

1 1/3 pound ground beef
1 small bag of peppered jerky
1 garlic clove, minced
2 scallions, sliced
1 Serrano pepper, seeded and minced
1 inch ginger root, grated
½ teaspoon nutmeg
1 teaspoon coarse black pepper
Salt to taste
1 ripe lime, juiced
4 green leaf lettuce leaves
4 Kaiser Rolls, halved

Salsa:
1 large papaya, seeded, peeled and diced
½ red bell pepper, seeded and diced
¼ red onion, finely chopped
2 tablespoons fresh cilantro, chopped
1 orange, juiced
Salt to taste

DIRECTIONS:

> Salsa: Mix all of the ingredients together and set aside.
> Mix the ground beef with the garlic, scallions, ginger, thyme, nutmeg, salt and pepper in a large bowl.
> Form the ground beef mixture into four 4 ounce balls. Create each ball into a patty by using the STUFF side of the burger press to push it down.
> Put the patties on the grill and cook for 6 minutes on each side.
> Serve: Place the patty on top of the bottom bun, top the patty with a lettuce leaf, two strips of peppered jerky and the salsa on top.

NEXT ON THE LIST!

Here's What You Do Now...

If you were please with our book then **please leave us a review on Amazon where you purchased this book!** www.amazon.com/dp/B076JDHW9Z In the world of an author who writes books independently, your reviews are not only touching but important so that we know you like the material we have prepared for "you" our audience! So leave us a review...we would love to see that you enjoyed our book!

If for any reason that you were less than happy with your experience then send me an email at **Feedback@Healthylifestylerecipes.org** and let me know how we can better your experience. We always come out with a few volumes of our books and will possibly be able to address some of your concerns. Do keep in mind that we strive to do our best to give you the highest quality of what "we the independent authors" pour our heart and tears into.

I am very happy to create new and exciting recipes and do appreciate your purchase. I thank you for your many great reviews and comments! With a warm heart! ~"Professional Chef and Burger Experts" Richard Erwin and Tasha :)

ABOUT THE AUTHORS

Richard Erwin and Tasha Spencer are a trained, self taught, private gourmet chefs (and burger experts) that has enjoyed their craft in the kitchens of many celebrities and exclusive events of Southern California and Texas. They both enjoy creating new recipes for an array of categories and writes recipes and books from their heart and soul to share with you!

FREE BOOKS!!

New Books, Pro Cooking Tips, & Recipes
Sent to Your Email

For our current readers...if you like receiving free books, pro tips and recipes to add to your collection, then this is for you! This is for promoting our new books before they come out, so you can review our new books and give us feed back when we launch them! This helps us determine how we can make our books better for you, our audience! Just go to the link below We will send you a complimentary book about once a month.

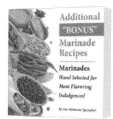

"Additional Marinades"
Yours FREE for signing up to Our List!

Get My Free Book

www.Healthylifestylerecipes.org/Freebook2review

RECIPE NOTES

_____

_____

_____

_____

_____

_____

_____

_____

_____

_____

_____

_____

_____

_____

_____

_____

RECIPE NOTES

RECIPE NOTES

_____

_____

_____

_____

_____

_____

_____

_____

_____

_____

_____

_____

_____

_____

_____

_____

Made in the USA
Middletown, DE
13 June 2018